Would You Rather

Game Book for Kids

This book belongs to:

_____

Would You Rather

Game Book for Kids

Welcome! We hope you and your imagination are ready. As we go through this book together, we will meet animals and enchanted creatures, ride hot air balloons, and take a rocket to the moon! And much, much more!

This Book includes silly and hilarious scenarios with jokes and Bonus Trivia questions to challenge your kids, their friends or your entire family.

Playtime can now be fun and educational! Plus, you can take this game wherever you go: road trips, sleepovers, parties, and more! Find out who has the better ideas and gives the best answers!

It is the perfect opportunity to develop critical thinking skills while having fun!

INSTRUCTIONS

1 The questions, or "scenarios", in this game are played in 4 levels, with 50 questions per level. Each level gets harder and sillier as you go!

2 You will need at least two players and pencils.

3 All the pages will have "Would You Rather" questions with two possible answers.

4 The youngest person will read the first question to start, but everyone can participatein taking turns reading later questions.

5 After the question is read aloud, the answering players answer as quickly as possible and give the reason for their decision.

INSTRUCTIONS

6 If someone doesn't answer fast enough, or picks both or no options, they don't get any points.

7 The player reading the question assigns 1 point to the best answer. Whoever gave the best answer wins for that question and the winner's name will be written in the box below the question.

8 Players will take turns reading the different pages in order from youngest to oldest.

9 At the end, the Players tally up their own answers to figure out how many points they earned. Whoever gets the most points is the winner!

10 There are also BONUS trivia questions at the end of the book to earn an additional 5 points each. The trivia answers are placed at the end of the book and can be cut so as to play as if it is a board game.

The most important rule is to be silly, creative, and have fun!

INDEX

EASY
p. 7

INTERMEDIATE
p. 33

ADVANCED
p. 59

SILLY
p.85

TRIVIA
p.111

TRIVIA ANSWERS
p.125

EASY

Participants:

Q 1

WOULD YOU RATHER

have wings and fly like a
hummingbird

sail in a hot air balloon?

Winner: | Points:

WOULD YOU RATHER

go on a treasure hunt with pirates

dig for dinosaurs with
archaeologists?

Winner: | Points:

Q 2

Participants:

Q/3

WOULD YOU RATHER

only eat cheese for one month

never get to eat cheese again?

Winner: Points:

WOULD YOU RATHER

have the memory of a goldfish

or of an elephant?

Q/4

Winner: Points:

Participants:

WOULD YOU RATHER

go stargazing

whale watching?

Winner: | Points:

WOULD YOU RATHER

be a ninja

a mermaid?

Winner: | Points:

Participants:

WOULD YOU RATHER

meet a genie

a fairy godmother?

Winner: Points:

WOULD YOU RATHER

be a lion tamer at the circus

a giraffe trainer at the zoo?

Winner: Points:

Participants:

Q/9

<u>WOULD YOU RATHER</u>

win a spelling bee

win a pie eating contest?

Winner: | Points:

<u>WOULD YOU RATHER</u>

have your skin turn blue

your hair turn pink?

Q/10

Winner: | Points:

12

Participants:

WOULD YOU RATHER

explore the
craters of the moon

a explore a live volcano?

Winner: Points:

Q / 11

WOULD YOU RATHER

ride a unicycle

a pogo stick?

Winner: Points:

Q / 12

Participants:

WOULD YOU RATHER

chase a tornado

climb the world's tallest tower?

Winner: | Points:

Q/13

WOULD YOU RATHER

never have to brush your teeth again

never have to brush your hair again?

Winner: | Points:

Q/14

Participants:

WOULD YOU RATHER

be friends with
a skeleton

a ghost?

Winner: | Points:

WOULD YOU RATHER

have a castle

a mansion?

Winner: | Points:

Participants:

WOULD YOU RATHER

ride the world's tallest roller coaster

the world's longest slide?

Winner: | Points:

Q/17

WOULD YOU RATHER

bake a million cookies

cook a million pancakes?

Winner: | Points:

Q/18

Participants:

Q 19

WOULD YOU RATHER

sing a song with your favorite celebrity

dance with your favorite celebrity?

Winner: Points:

WOULD YOU RATHER

get stung by a scorpion

a bumblebee?

Q 20

Winner: Points:

Participants:

WOULD YOU RATHER

own a zoo

an amusement park?

Winner: | Points:

WOULD YOU RATHER

make a peanut
butter sandwich with strawberry jelly

grape jelly?

Winner: | Points:

Participants:

WOULD YOU RATHER

make s'mores
at a campfire

cotton candy at the circus?

Winner: Points:

Q 23

WOULD YOU RATHER

go to the movie theater

go shopping

Winner: Points:

Q 24

Participants:

WOULD YOU RATHER

have 100 pairs of shoes

100 hats?

Winner: Points:

WOULD YOU RATHER

have summer forever

winter forever?

Winner: Points:

Participants:

WOULD YOU RATHER

switch places for a day with your best friend

with a dog?

Winner: Points:

Q
27

WOULD YOU RATHER

lay eggs like a chicken

have a pouch like a kangaroo?

Winner: Points:

Q
28

Participants:

WOULD YOU RATHER

eat pancakes for the rest of your life

waffles?

Winner: Points:

Q/29

WOULD YOU RATHER

control electricity

glow in the dark like a firefly?

Winner: Points:

Q/30

Participants:

WOULD YOU RATHER

roll around in the mud like a pig

relax in a birdbath?

Winner: Points:

WOULD YOU RATHER

only be able to use a fork to
eat forever

a spoon?

Winner: Points:

Participants:

Q/33

WOULD YOU RATHER

learn to juggle

tightrope walk?

Winner: | Points:

WOULD YOU RATHER

live in an igloo

Q/34

a cave?

Winner: | Points:

Participants:

Q 35

WOULD YOU RATHER

ride a unicorn

a dragon?

Winner: Points:

WOULD YOU RATHER

live with a pack
of wolves

a waddle of penguins

Q 36

Winner: Points:

Participants:

WOULD YOU RATHER

a surprise party thrown for you

throw a surprise party for your friend?

Winner: Points:

Q 37

WOULD YOU RATHER

paint a picture

make a sculpture?

Winner: Points:

Q 38

Participants:

WOULD YOU RATHER

snuggle a hedgehog

a panda bear?

Winner: Points:

WOULD YOU RATHER

be able to see in the dark

breathe underwater?

Winner: Points:

Participants:

WOULD YOU RATHER

cover yourself
in stickers

 or

bandaids?

Winner: Points:

Q
41

WOULD YOU RATHER

have webbed
fingers

 or

webbed toes?

Winner: Points:

Q
42

Participants:

WOULD YOU RATHER

have a beak

 or

feathers?

Winner: Points:

Q 43

WOULD YOU RATHER

have a tail

 or

antlers?

Winner: Points:

Q 44

Participants:

WOULD YOU RATHER

brain freeze from food that's
too cold

burn your tongue from food that's
too hot?

Winner: Points:

Q/45

WOULD YOU RATHER

visit the
North Pole

the South Pole?

Q/46

Winner: Points:

Participants:

WOULD YOU RATHER

ride a camel

a dolphin?

Winner: Points:

WOULD YOU RATHER

draw with
colored pencils

crayons?

Winner: Points:

Participants:

WOULD YOU RATHER

watch fireworks

parade?

Winner:　　　　　　Points:

WOULD YOU RATHER

discover

a mummy

an alien?

Winner:　　　　　　Points:

Q/49

Q/50

Participants:

WOULD YOU RATHER

make a wish

in a well

a wish upon a star

Winner: | Points:

WOULD YOU RATHER

be the President of the

United States for a week

King of your own island forever?

Winner: | Points:

Participants:

<u>WOULD YOU RATHER</u>

invent

something new

 or

discover something ancient?

Winner: Points:

<u>WOULD YOU RATHER</u>

be able to control the weather

 or

time travel?

Winner: Points:

Participants:

WOULD YOU RATHER

study
the bones

the brain?

Winner: Points:

WOULD YOU RATHER

pick your own apples from
an apple orchard

pick your own strawberries from a
strawberry field?

Winner: Points:

Participants:

WOULD YOU RATHER

go bowling with bigfoot

scuba diving with the Loch Ness Monster?

Winner: Points:

Q/57

WOULD YOU RATHER

build an igloo with snow outside

a fort with pillows and blankets inside?

Winner: Points:

Q/58

Participants:

Q 59

WOULD YOU RATHER

celebrate your birthday
every month

your favorite holiday?

Winner:

Points:

WOULD YOU RATHER

win a teddy bear from
the carnival

a goldfish?

Q 60

Winner:

Points:

Participants:

WOULD YOU RATHER

spend a month in Europe

in Asia?

Winner: Points:

Q/61

WOULD YOU RATHER

have a robot to do all
your chores

homework?

Winner: Points:

Q/62

Participants:

WOULD YOU RATHER

have to yell every time you talk

 or

whisper?

Q/63

Winner: Points:

WOULD YOU RATHER

have better
handwriting

 or

be better at math?

Q/64

Winner: Points:

Participants:

WOULD YOU RATHER

be in a movie

in a play?

Winner:

Points:

WOULD YOU RATHER

dress fancy
all day

wear pajamas all day?

Winner:

Points:

Participants:

WOULD YOU RATHER

be a chef

a baker?

Winner: | Points:

Q / 67

WOULD YOU RATHER

carry a
backpack

a briefcase?

Winner: | Points:

Q / 68

Participants:

Q 69

WOULD YOU RATHER

go on vacation with
your family

friends?

Winner: Points:

WOULD YOU RATHER

take a nap
with a koala

a sloth?

Q 70

Winner: Points:

Participants:

Q 71

WOULD YOU RATHER

fight a zombie

a werewolf?

Winner: Points:

WOULD YOU RATHER

be as wise
as an owl

as brave as a lion?

Q 72

Winner: Points:

Participants:

Q/73

WOULD YOU RATHER

do yoga with a flamingo

try boxing with a kangaroo?

Winner: | Points:

WOULD YOU RATHER

put together a 500 piece puzzle

solve a tricky riddle?

Q/74

Winner: | Points:

Participants:

Q/75

<u>WOULD YOU RATHER</u>

learn how to make a candle

make a bar of soap?

Winner: Points:

<u>WOULD YOU RATHER</u>

have two brains

three stomachs?

Q/76

Winner: Points:

Participants:

Q/77

WOULD YOU RATHER

write 100 letters

receive 100 letters in the mail?

Winner: Points:

WOULD YOU RATHER

make a
snow angel

jump into a pile of leaves?

Q/78

Winner: Points:

Participants:

Q/79

WOULD YOU RATHER

build a sandcastle

go scuba diving?

Winner:

Points:

WOULD YOU RATHER

explore a
haunted house

explore an Egyptian tomb?

Winner:

Points:

Q/80

Participants:

Q
81

WOULD YOU RATHER

knit a sweater

sew a quilt?

Winner:

Points:

WOULD YOU RATHER

create your own board game

invent a new sport?

Q
82

Winner:

Points:

Participants:

Q 83

WOULD YOU RATHER

have breakfast for dinner
every day

eat dessert first before
every meal?

Winner:

Points:

WOULD YOU RATHER

go camping on Mars

in the rainforest?

Q 84

Winner:

Points:

Participants:

WOULD YOU RATHER

pick your own flowers

go hunting for mushrooms?

Winner: Points:

Q 85

WOULD YOU RATHER

make friends with a huge giant

a little elf?

Winner: Points:

Q 86

Participants:

WOULD YOU RATHER

be the pilot of
an airplane

the captain of a ship?

Winner:

Points:

Q 87

WOULD YOU RATHER

see the
pyramids of Egypt

the Great Wall of China?

Winner:

Points:

Q 88

Participants:

Q 89

WOULD YOU RATHER

be covered in fur

scales?

Winner:

Points:

WOULD YOU RATHER

follow a map

a compass when you are lost?

Q 90

Winner:

Points:

Participants:

Q / 91

WOULD YOU RATHER

watch the
sun rise

or

the sun set?

Winner: Points:

WOULD YOU RATHER

chase
butterflies

or

fireflies?

Q / 92

Winner: Points:

Participants:

WOULD YOU RATHER

have talons like a dragon

or

paws like a dog?

Winner: Points:

Q/93

WOULD YOU RATHER

compete in the "Iditarod" race
with sled dogs

or

earn a gold medal in the Olympics?

Winner: Points:

Q/94

Participants:

WOULD YOU RATHER

live inside the mouth of a whale

inside the chamber of a bat cave?

Q/95

Winner: | Points:

WOULD YOU RATHER

collect stamps

rocks?

Q/96

Winner: | Points:

Participants:

WOULD YOU RATHER

go on a short
boat trip

a long car trip?

Winner: Points:

WOULD YOU RATHER

take a bath
with hippos

take a shower from an
elephant's trunk?

Winner: Points:

Participants:

Q 99

WOULD YOU RATHER

have a water
balloon fight

silly string battle?

Winner: | Points:

WOULD YOU RATHER

play a prank on
your parents

your friends?

Q 100

Winner: | Points:

ADVANCED

Participants:

Q 101

WOULD YOU RATHER

move as slowly as a turtle but
always be on time

move as fast as a cheetah but
always run late?

Winner: | Points:

WOULD YOU RATHER

speak every
language in the world

read every book in the world?

Q 102

Winner: | Points:

60

Participants:

Q 103

WOULD YOU RATHER

be able to talk to animals

trees?

Winner:

Points:

WOULD YOU RATHER

have no
reflection

no shadow?

Q 104

Winner:

Points:

Participants:

Q 105

WOULD YOU RATHER

never get
sick again

have the ability to make other
people better?

Winner: Points:

WOULD YOU RATHER

be a
superhero

a super villain?

Q 106

Winner: Points:

Participants:

WOULD YOU RATHER

solve
world hunger

or

negotiate world peace?

Winner: | Points:

Q / 107

WOULD YOU RATHER

forget
your ABCs

or

forget how to count to 10?

Winner: | Points:

Q / 108

Participants:

Q/109

WOULD YOU RATHER

see your face
on a dollar bill

 or

on your favorite cereal box?

Winner: Points:

WOULD YOU RATHER

discover
a new color

 or

a new word?

Q/110

Winner: Points:

Participants:

WOULD YOU RATHER

teach an
alien how to talk

teach a mermaid how to walk?

Winner: Points:

Q/111

WOULD YOU RATHER

protect the
environment

help endangered animals?

Winner: Points:

Q/112

Participants:

WOULD YOU RATHER

never have to do laundry again

 or

never have to clean your room?

Winner: Points:

Q 113

WOULD YOU RATHER

be a mystery
detective

 or

a lion tamer?

Winner: Points:

Q 114

Participants:

Q 115

<u>WOULD YOU RATHER</u>

only eat soup
forever

only sandwiches?

Winner: Points:

<u>WOULD YOU RATHER</u>

have to rhyme every
line you say

sing every time you talk?

Q 116

Winner: Points:

Participants:

Q 117

WOULD YOU RATHER

turn into a
picture book

a cartoon?

Winner: Points:

WOULD YOU RATHER

have no fears

be the smartest person alive?

Q 118

Winner: Points:

Participants:

Q / 119

WOULD YOU RATHER

have a
bigger brain

a bigger heart?

Winner: Points:

WOULD YOU RATHER

be
shorter

taller?

Q / 120

Winner: Points:

Participants:

Q 121

WOULD YOU RATHER

be 10
years older

10 years younger?

Winner: Points:

WOULD YOU RATHER

spin in circles until you're dizzy

experience zero gravity in space?

Q 122

Winner: Points:

Participants:

WOULD YOU RATHER

have a button that makes
people dance

 or

a button that makes people
go to sleep?

Winner: | Points:

Q
123

WOULD YOU RATHER

give people
good dreams

 or

nightmares?

Winner: | Points:

Q
124

Participants:

WOULD YOU RATHER

get up
early

stay up late?

Winner: Points:

WOULD YOU RATHER

be handcuffed to your sibling for
24 hours

your best friend?

Winner: Points:

Participants:

WOULD YOU RATHER

have unlimited snacks

unlimited internet?

Winner: Points:

Q 127

WOULD YOU RATHER

roll down the hill like a log

crabwalk down the hill sideways?

Winner: Points:

Q 128

Participants:

WOULD YOU RATHER

hibernate like
a bear

hide your head in the sand like
an ostrich?

Winner: | Points:

Q 129

WOULD YOU RATHER

have a twin

have a robot clone?

Q 130

Winner: | Points:

Participants:

Q 131

WOULD YOU RATHER

never learn how to ride a bike

never learn how to drive a car?

Winner: | Points:

WOULD YOU RATHER

stay a
kid forever

get really, really old?

Q 132

Winner: | Points:

Participants:

WOULD YOU RATHER

have ice powers

or

fire powers?

Winner: Points:

Q 133

WOULD YOU RATHER

be able to make things really big

or

really tiny?

Winner: Points:

Q 134

Participants:

WOULD YOU RATHER

transform into a magical creature

your favorite wild animal?

Winner: Points:

WOULD YOU RATHER

have a pet turtle

a pet squirrel?

Winner: Points:

Participants:

WOULD YOU RATHER

bring your
toys to life

turn into a toy?

Winner: | Points:

Q 137

WOULD YOU RATHER

turn
into a fruit

a vegetable?

Winner: | Points:

Q 138

Participants:

Q 139

WOULD YOU RATHER

wear a crown

a cape every day?

Winner: | Points:

WOULD YOU RATHER

live in a bird's nest

a turtle's shell?

Q 140

Winner: | Points:

Participants:

WOULD YOU RATHER

be loud like a lion

sneaky like a fox?

Winner: | Points:

Q 141

WOULD YOU RATHER

know the ending to every movie

every book?

Winner: | Points:

Q 142

Participants:

WOULD YOU RATHER

know everybody's secrets

have one very big secret that no one can ever discover?

Winner: | Points:

Q 143

WOULD YOU RATHER

have a waterbed

a bunk bed?

Q 144

Winner: | Points:

Participants:

Q 145

WOULD YOU RATHER

have the best
hiding spot in hide'n'seek

be the best finder?

Winner: Points:

WOULD YOU RATHER

wear a shirt
that's too small

pants that are too big?

Q 146

Winner: Points:

Participants:

WOULD YOU RATHER

find the end of a rainbow

float on a rain cloud?

Winner: Points:

WOULD YOU RATHER

dance in the rain

jump in mud puddles?

Winner: Points:

Participants:

Q 149

WOULD YOU RATHER

be an art teacher

a gym teacher?

Winner: Points:

WOULD YOU RATHER

go to the grocery store

a car wash?

Q 150

Winner: Points:

SILLY

Participants:

Q 151

WOULD YOU RATHER

have to wear a clown nose
every day

clown shoes?

Winner:　　　　Points:

WOULD YOU RATHER

have broccoli taste like donuts

lima beans taste like candy?

Q 152

Winner:　　　　Points:

Participants:

WOULD YOU RATHER

jump into a pool of Jell-O

a pool of mashed potatoes?

Winner: Points:

WOULD YOU RATHER

have cotton candy trees

marshmallow flowers?

Winner: Points:

Participants:

WOULD YOU RATHER

have a talking parrot

a mind reading dog as a pet?

Q
155

Winner: Points:

WOULD YOU RATHER

have the tongue of a cow

a frog?

Q
156

Winner: Points:

Participants:

WOULD YOU RATHER

only be able to
talk backwards

talk like a pirate?

Winner: | Points:

WOULD YOU RATHER

eat ketchup ice cream

chicken noodle soup yogurt?

Winner: | Points:

Participants:

WOULD YOU RATHER

grow a mustache

shave all your hair off?

Winner: Points:

WOULD YOU RATHER

brush an alligator's teeth

comb a monkey's hair?

Winner: Points:

Participants:

WOULD YOU RATHER

have spaghetti for hair

 or

a meatball for a nose?

Q 161

Winner:

Points:

WOULD YOU RATHER

forget to wear shoes to school

 or

forget to bring your homework?

Q 162

Winner:

Points:

Participants:

WOULD YOU RATHER

hug a hedgehog

give a high five to each of an octopus' tentacles?

Q 163

Winner: Points:

WOULD YOU RATHER

make the world's biggest pizza

biggest cheeseburger?

Q 164

Winner: Points:

Participants:

WOULD YOU RATHER

walk on your hands

take a scooter
everywhere you go?

Winner: | Points:

Q 165

WOULD YOU RATHER

do a cartwheel

a backflip?

Winner: | Points:

Q 166

Participants:

Q 167

WOULD YOU RATHER

play jump rope with a long
piece of spaghetti

play four square with
a meatball?

Winner: Points:

WOULD YOU RATHER

sleep in a coffin like a vampire

in a tree like a sloth?

Q 168

Winner: Points:

Participants:

Q 169

WOULD YOU RATHER

go to a zebra's birthday party

a turtle's birthday party?

Winner: Points:

WOULD YOU RATHER

have rulers for arms

rulers for legs?

Q 170

Winner: Points:

Participants:

WOULD YOU RATHER

have permanent goosebumps

grow feathers every time
you get scared?

Winner: | Points:

WOULD YOU RATHER

cry tears of orange juice

sweat drops of apple juice?

Winner: | Points:

Participants:

WOULD YOU RATHER

sparkle in the sun

glow in the dark?

Winner: | Points:

Q
173

WOULD YOU RATHER

have rainbow hair

rainbow skin?

Winner: | Points:

Q
174

Participants:

Q 175

WOULD YOU RATHER

bring a dinosaur back to life

bring a dodo bird
back from extinction?

Winner: Points:

WOULD YOU RATHER

be sneezed on by an elephant

by a butterfly?

Q 176

Winner: Points:

Participants:

WOULD YOU RATHER

be next to a burping ogre

a spraying skunk?

Winner: Points:

WOULD YOU RATHER

drink an evil witch's potion

get kidnapped by a super villain?

Winner: Points:

Participants:

WOULD YOU RATHER

go bowling with a pumpkin

 or

with a watermelon?

Winner: Points:

Q 179

WOULD YOU RATHER

play catch with
a water balloon

 or

with an egg?

Winner: Points:

Q 180

Participants:

Q 181

WOULD YOU RATHER

be stuck in a maze with

a mouse

with a scarecrow?

Winner: Points:

WOULD YOU RATHER

spin in circles

on a tire swing

in a flying saucer?

Q 182

Winner: Points:

Participants:

WOULD YOU RATHER

touch moldy cheese

 or

touch rotten eggs?

Winner: Points:

WOULD YOU RATHER

have cotton
candy hair

 or

licorice hair?

Winner: Points:

Participants:

WOULD YOU RATHER

have a house made of candy

 or

clothes made of candy?

Winner: Points:

WOULD YOU RATHER

turn your pets
into humans

 or

turn your best friends into pets?

Winner: Points:

Participants:

**Q
187**

WOULD YOU RATHER

talk like a chipmunk

talk like a robot?

Winner: Points:

WOULD YOU RATHER

have extra ears

eyes in the back of your head?

**Q
188**

Winner: Points:

Participants:

WOULD YOU RATHER

eat a hamburger with
no cheese

or no bun?

Winner: Points:

WOULD YOU RATHER

launch a potato

a bell pepper from a slingshot?

Winner: Points:

Participants:

WOULD YOU RATHER

play hide'n'seek in an
enchanted forest

a massive desert?

Winner: Points:

WOULD YOU RATHER

be turned
into a snowman

a statue?

Winner: Points:

Participants:

Q 193

WOULD YOU RATHER

make a million
paper airplanes

a million paper cranes?

Winner: | Points:

WOULD YOU RATHER

have teeth made of
candy corn

real corn?

Q 194

Winner: | Points:

Participants:

WOULD YOU RATHER

have fingers made of carrots

made of celery?

Winner: | Points:

WOULD YOU RATHER

have a tea party with a lady bug

a praying mantis?

Winner: | Points:

Participants:

WOULD YOU RATHER

smash a guitar

smash a piano?

Winner: Points:

WOULD YOU RATHER

milk a cow

milk a goat?

Winner: Points:

Participants:

WOULD YOU RATHER

swim in a river made
of chocolate milk

made of soda?

Winner: Points:

Q 199

WOULD YOU RATHER

always have to
wear floaties

goggles?

Winner: Points:

Q 200

TRIVIA

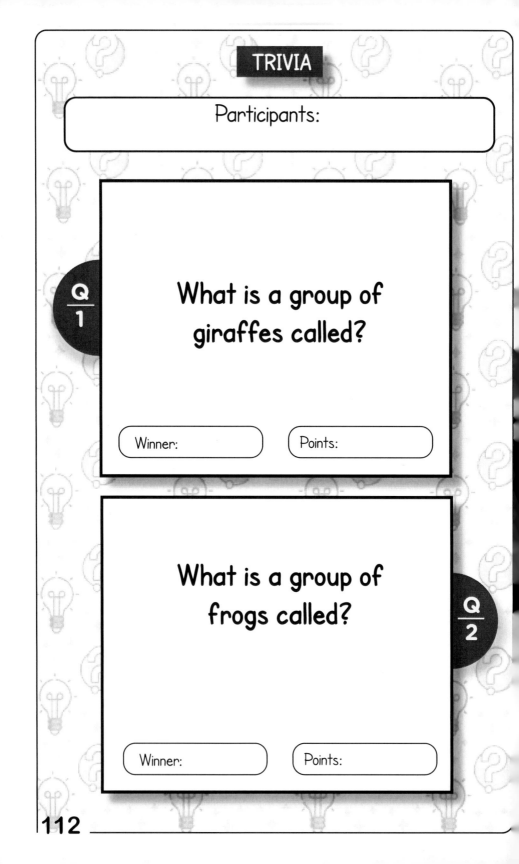

Participants:

Q/1

What is a group of giraffes called?

Winner:

Points:

What is a group of frogs called?

Q/2

Winner:

Points:

Participants:

Q 3

If LEGO bricks were stacked in a single column, how many would it take to reach the Moon from the surface of Earth?

Winner: Points:

What dinosaur looked very similar to a rhino?

Q 4

Winner: Points:

TRIVIA

Participants:

Q/5

What are you afraid of if you have arachnophobia?

Winner: | Points:

Q/6

What are you afraid of if you have triskaidekaphobia?

Winner: | Points:

114

Participants:

Q/7

Where does dim sum come from?

Winner: Points:

Q/8

Where do enchiladas come from?

Winner: Points:

Participants:

Q/9

Where does sushi come from?

Winner: Points:

Do you use more muscles to smile or frown?

Q/10

Winner: Points:

Participants:

Q/11

Which scientist discovered gravity?

Winner: Points:

Where was King Tut buried?

Q/12

Winner: Points:

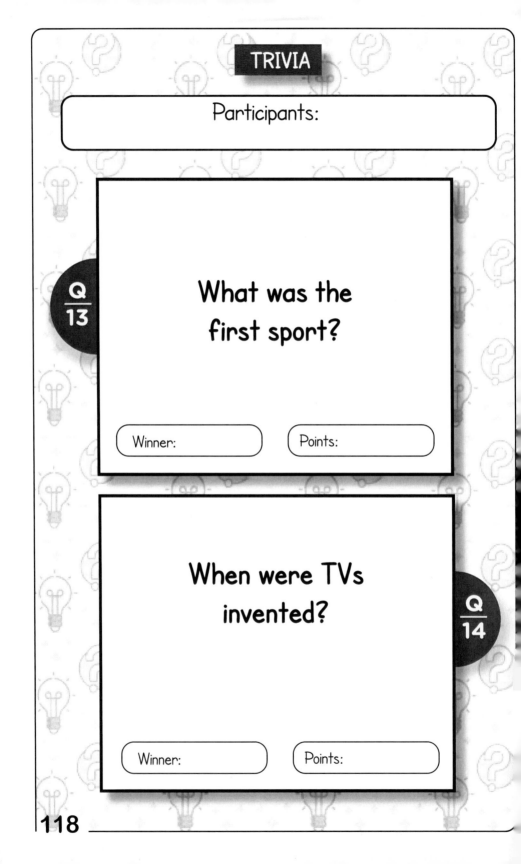

TRIVIA

Participants:

Q/13

What was the
first sport?

Winner:

Points:

When were TVs
invented?

Q/14

Winner:

Points:

118

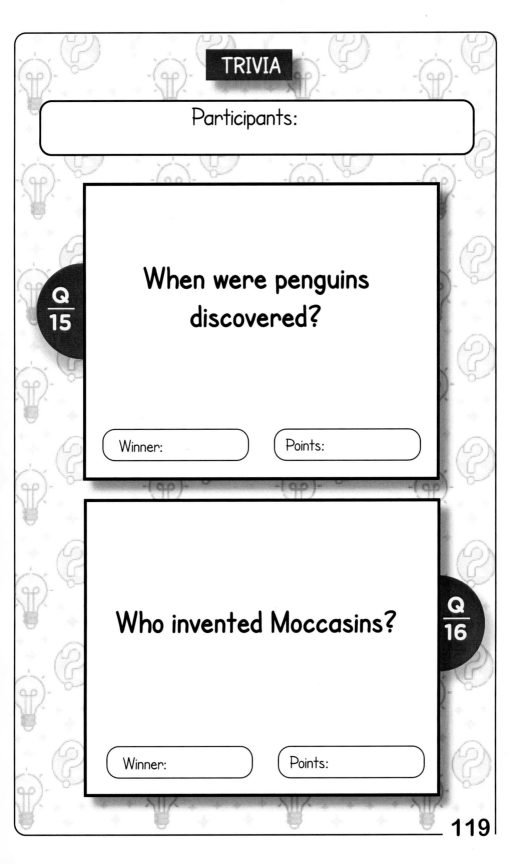

TRIVIA

Participants:

Q 15

When were penguins discovered?

Winner: Points:

Q 16

Who invented Moccasins?

Winner: Points:

Participants:

What are three types
of clouds?

Winner: Points:

How many teeth do
grown ups have?

Winner: Points:

Participants:

Q 19

When were movie theaters invented?

Winner:　　　　　Points:

Q 20

What is the most popular dog breed in the world?

Winner:　　　　　Points:

Participants:

Q / 21

How much does an elephant weigh?

Winner: Points:

What are 3 forms of precipitation?

Q / 22

Winner: Points:

Participants:

Q 23

What process do plants use to make food?

Winner: Points:

Q 24

How many potentially active volcanoes are there in the world?

Winner: Points:

Participants:

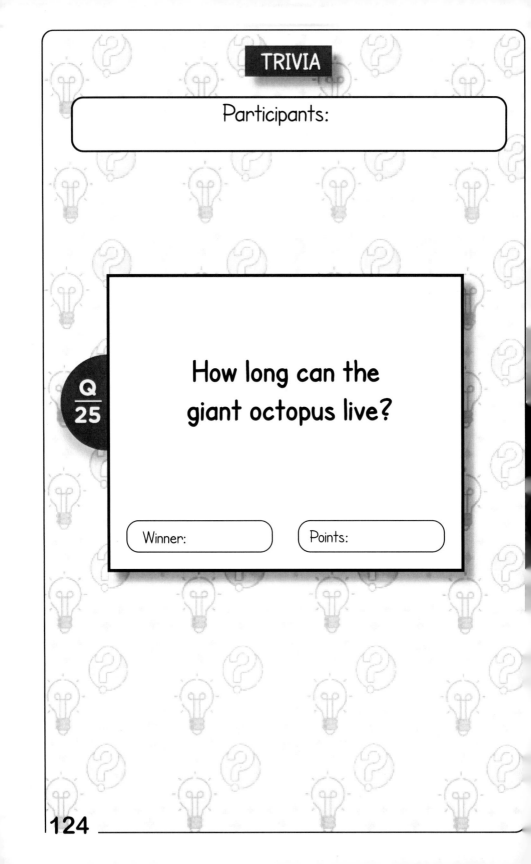

$\frac{Q}{25}$

How long can the giant octopus live?

Winner:

Points:

Q1

Q2

Q3

Q4

Q5

Q6

Q7

Q8

AN ARMY

A TOWER

TRICERATOPS

40 BILLION

THE NUMBER 13

SPIDERS

MEXICO

CHINA

TRIVIA ANSWERS

Q9

Q10

Q11

Q12

Q13

Q14

Q15

Q16

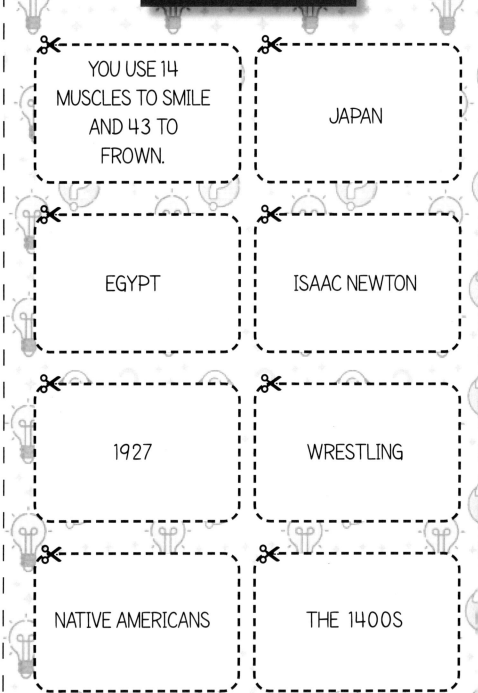

YOU USE 14 MUSCLES TO SMILE AND 43 TO FROWN.

JAPAN

EGYPT

ISAAC NEWTON

1927

WRESTLING

NATIVE AMERICANS

THE 1400S

Q17

Q18

Q19

Q20

Q21

Q22

Q23

Q24

32

STRATUS, CIRRUS, CUMULONIMBUS

LABRADOR RETRIEVER

THE 1900S

SNOW, RAIN, HAIL

5000-14,000 LBS

1500

PHOTOSYNTHESIS

Q25

NOTES

5 YEARS

NOTES

CONGRATULATIONS!

You're truly amazing! I am sure there are some obstacles along the way; it was great you persisted through and finished the job!

If you want to continue with more activities, just send me an email to support@kidsactivitybooks.org and I will send you some for free.

My name is Jennifer Trace and I hope you found this workbook helpful and fun. If you have any suggestions about how to improve this book, changes to make or how to make it more useful, please let me know.

If you like this book, would you be so kind and leave me a review on Amazon.

Thank you very much!
Jennifer Trace

Congratulations
Trivia Star:

THE BEST!

Date:_____   Signed:_____

Made in United States
North Haven, CT
03 August 2022

22155650R00074